ACT AGAINST BULLYING

Situational Monologues for Children

Louise Burfitt-Dons

Printed in the UK
First Printing: Aug 2002
New Century Drama/Theatre

ISBN 13: 9780953852246
ISBN 10: 0953852245

for Act Against Bullying

CONTENTS

INTRODUCTION

Since these situational monologues were first published in 2002 they have been used by hundreds of schools and organisations who have found them indispensable in countering bullying and increasing overall empathy amongst students. In the text they are labelled for girls (G) or boys (B) though many can be transposed easily. The final set scene pieces have been added recently to cover social media, cyberbullying, sexting, and parental abuse.

Role-play should be followed by student/teacher discussion on the implications of the situations covered in the set of monologues. Research shows that certain students will seldom take the initiative to bully another student, but will easily 'go along' with crowd behaviour out of fear or disengagement. They are unaware of how their tacit involvement can cause pain not only to the target of bullying but also to themselves. It is in this area that the use of these situational monologues can be most effective.

Spellings and colloquial expressions may vary depending on country, i.e. the spelling of colour in the US is 'color', organise is 'organize' etc. For more advice and information on how to tackle all forms of bullying please check out the website at www.actagainstbullying.org

SHE IGNORED ME (G)

When I saw Frankie in geography, I asked her why she was ignoring me. And why she ran away from me in the playground. My heart was beating that hard. I really didn't want to ask her. Just in case she said she didn't like me anymore. 'Why did you run away from me?' Frankie looked straight ahead. Then she turned to look the other way and turned her back on me. She got up and started grabbing hold of Amy. Then they walked off. I could see Amy saying something to her. It felt really awful. I started to cry and Frankie looked a bit embarrassed. Another girl said it was Amy's fault. She'd got all my friends to run away from me. They had to do so. Otherwise they wouldn't be in the group anymore. Everyone wants to be in the group. Me too.

PARTNERS (G)

When you go into the classroom in the morning, there are always people screaming and running around. I just want to stay at the back and be on my own. The worse time is when you have to have a partner. And you know no one will pick you. It makes you feel really bad like everyone hates you. I told my mum, and she said to go and ask someone to be my partner first. But I tried that once. It was in a cooking lesson. We were making cakes, and we had to be with someone else. I asked this girl, 'Will you be my partner?' and she said, 'Yes'. I was really happy. Then when we went to the table, she suddenly said 'I don't want to be your partner any more' and ran off and joined another girl. I was left on my own and the teacher told me off. 'I said to get into partners' she said. I never asked anybody again. My mum says I'm shy, but I'm not really. It's just I don't want that to happen again. It was horrible.

NEW CLOTHES (G)

No one wants to be with me at school. When I told my mum she said. 'Maybe it's because you don't wear the right things.' So she took me out to buy new clothes. She's really nice, my mum. She didn't have to do that. She bought me these new jeans and stuff that was really expensive. When I wore them on Mufti, everyone just stared at me. No one said anything. Not one word. So I asked Sarah, 'Do you like what I'm wearing?' She said, 'Yeah', but not like she meant it. Then her friend said, 'Just because you've got new clothes doesn't mean anything.' I told Sarah that my mum had bought them to help me get accepted. 'Buying new things doesn't make you cool, stupid' someone said. They said really horrid things like, 'You're bragging'. And 'Just because you've got some new jeans doesn't mean you have to tell everyone, do you?' But I wasn't doing it to show off. I wish I hadn't worn them now. Anyway, I look stupid in new clothes. When I told my mum she hugged me. She looked really hurt. 'Can we take them back to the shop? I asked. She just told me to stop crying.

THEY RAN OFF (G)

The crowd were being really mean to me—even Zoe. And I thought she was my friend. Every time I went up to them in the playground they ran away from me screaming 'She's coming. Quick. Run.' Zoe running away was the worst thing. I didn't know what to do. Whether to follow them or what. So I ran after them to ask if I could play. They ran off again. Amy said, 'Go away,' really fiercely. 'We want to be on our own,' she said with this horrid face. 'We're talking privately' they shouted at me and I wasn't supposed to listen. I went and sat on the bench. I thought I was going to cry, but I didn't. I knew that if I did a teacher would come and ask why. If I told her the group was avoiding me she'd make me go and play with someone I don't like. And Amy and Zoe would get into trouble. So when the teacher came over to me I pretended I was playing hide and seek with them. Counting to 100.

PRESENTS (G)

The bad thing about being bullied by the gang is that you can't tell anyone, really. If you do, then they'll never speak to you anymore. Or you will be forced by the teachers to play with all the bad people. So it is better to be bullied by them than not be with them at all. And yet every night I cry when I go to sleep. I wish they wouldn't be so mean and frightening. I am always trying to find ways of keeping in with them. Mummy used to buy these little presents for me to give them. She didn't like doing it. I said, 'Everyone does it.' It was just to help me keep in with them. I gave June her bracelet, and she said 'Okay, you can sit here today.' The next day she was horrible again. Mum says I can't buy any more things for them so I just have to hope they will be nice to me one day. Either that, or June will fight with someone else and then she'll want me back in the crowd again to be on her side. But it's June who is the problem. If it wasn't for her, we would be the happiest gang of girls in the world. It's always June that ruins things. And yet she's still the leader of the gang. It doesn't make sense at all.

THE BULLY (B)

He is one of the coolest people. He has always got to have the latest thing. I went into school with the watch I got for my birthday. I was so pleased with it. He said, 'Oh look you've got one of those too. Cool.' It felt so good. At last I had something cool. Then he said,' Anyway I've got three of those at home. They are not the latest thing anymore.' And he walked off. But other times he can be really good fun. That's the trouble. Everyone wants to be around him because he's always the one at the centre of things. He brags a lot though my mum says a lot of it's made up. He is always having fights and calling people the 'b' word. I think everyone is really frightened of him because he's always putting people down. 'That won't work you dummy,' He said to Ethan about his science project. And you know what? If we'd done it Ethan's way then we would have won the whole competition. He doesn't care about work at all. He calls everyone who does weird. And no one wants to be called weird. I was called a weird, fat idiot one day because I stood up to him. But the trouble is that if you don't keep in with him, you will not be able to play with your other friends. Because he is the leader of the group. I wish he wasn't such a bully.

PICKING TEAMS (G)

In games the teacher asked Joanne and Kate to pick teams. They had to stand at the front. At first it wasn't too bad. Joanne picked Kirsty first, but then they're really good friends. Kate is always with Jane. But then it got to the end, and it became really embarrassing. I was trying not to cry. Kate looked at me and I thought she was going to pick me but Jane said 'No, pick Elaine. Elaine.' So she did. And then all the others were picked, and it was just the two of us left. Joanne picked Emily and so I was left to go to Kate's team and they all looked disappointed. I started to cry. I was trying not to, but it's horrible when no one wants you at all. Kate said, 'I wanted to pick you. Honest I did.' After that they weren't too bad. I wish the teacher would pick the teams. Then I wouldn't always be left to the end because everyone stares at you like you've got something wrong with you.

NICE PEOPLE (G)

Sandy is really nice, but no one likes her because everyone picks on her. Well, it's not that they don't like her in herself but they don't want to be like her. So they stay away from her. It's not fair, really. I am sure Sandy would have friends if she wasn't always picked on by Gemma. She doesn't do anything bad at all and she can be really, really nice. But it's just no one will play with her. Gemma's always talking about her in front of her to hurt her. Sandy tried to stand up to Gemma once. She said, 'Please don't talk about me like that' but the others all laughed. Everyone does it, picks on her. I don't know why, really. When they are away from Gemma they say things like, 'Gemma is really mean. I don't think Sandy should be picked on all the time. She was really nice to me at break when I hurt myself.' Then the next minute they are doing it as well. They will be hanging around together and then Gemma says, 'God I hate Sandy. She is so awful. Do you like her?' And then they all say 'Oh, no. I hate her too.' I ask them sometimes, ' Do you really hate Sandy or is it only because Gemma does.' And they can't answer. How would they like it if it were happening to them?

POSH (G)

My mum told me to ignore them but I can't. Anyway, you can't ignore them because you have to sit with them at lunch and do lessons with them. When you go into the classroom, they are always there staring at you. It makes you feel really awful inside. Mum said that I had to learn to answer them back, but it is very hard because you feel like crying if you do. I did it once—cried—and everyone in the class crowded round me. 'Don't cry'. But then it all started up again. They say no one likes me because I'm too posh. Tina said 'It must be awful having to do manners all the time' but I said 'No, it isn't, really.' Then she went quiet. No one said anything and then they all went off and left me and put their arms around one another. My mother said it was a good thing to be called posh, but she doesn't understand. They don't mean it as a good thing. 'Well then what about Posh Spice?' says Mum? And I told her it wasn't that type of posh that they meant. It wasn't a good thing. Posh Spice was cool and I'm not cool. And every night when I go to sleep I pray that I can make a friend. But it is impossible when nobody likes you.

TEACHER'S PET (G)

There's a girl in the class who is a sort of teacher's pet. Cheryl. She's good at everything, really. And she always does her homework. She even swats for exams and the teachers all say she is polite. I suppose in some ways it would be nice to be like her, to hand in your books and have them come back with big ticks. But then everyone talks about her behind her back. One person started it off at first and then everyone else in the class joined in. They wrote a rude word on the front cover of her English book and tied her laces together. That sort of thing. They do really mean things to her sometimes and call her 'strange'. The trouble is that if you take her side then you will be slagged off too. They all say 'She might be clever, but no one likes her. Everyone really hates her'. My mum said that that happened to her at school. She was bullied because she worked hard. But then when she left she got a good job and now everyone looks up to her. Someone told me that I was only 'in' with the crowd because they reckoned my mum was super cool with her nice house and car. I wonder if I would still be 'in' if they knew that my mother was once a teacher's pet like Cheryl?

DESKS (G)

No one wants to sit beside Chloe so when the bell goes everybody rushes to a desk next to someone they like. Then, if we have to change classrooms, before the bell goes, it's like 'Get out of my way' to people so that you can rush to get to the next room first. It's all because no one wants to be left with Chloe. At first I felt really sorry for her so I asked her to sit beside me in French. But then she wanted to be with me every lesson. It was awful. I said, 'Look, I can sit with you once in a while but right now I want to go off with my other friends.' And she looked really upset. Nobody else sits with her at all. And she's not that bad, really. She has these irritating habits that even the teachers don't like. She pulls these silly faces and keeps sticking her fingers in her ears and rattling things on the desk. And the problem is that if you sit with her, then none of your friends will speak to you for the rest of the day. They won't let you join in their group because she's sitting with you and they don't want her in their crowd. Then you might never get back with your friends again.

THE BULLY (G)

She is one of the coolest people and she has always got to have the latest thing. I went into school with the watch I got for my birthday. I was so pleased with it. She said, 'Oh look you've got one of those too. Cool.' It felt so good. At last I had something cool. Then she said,' Anyway I've got three of those at home. They are not the latest thing anymore.' And she walked off. But other times she can be really good fun. That's the trouble. Everyone wants to be around her because she is always the one at the discos and at the centre of things. She brags a lot though my mum says a lot of it's made up. She is always having fights and calling people the 'b' word. I think everyone is really frightened of her because she is always putting people down. 'That won't work, you dummy,' she said to Jenny about her science project. And you know what? If we'd done it Jenny's way then we would have won the whole competition. She doesn't care about work at all and she calls everyone who does 'weird'. And no one wants to be called weird. I was called a weird, fat idiot one day because I stood up to her. I cried all night after that. But the trouble is that if you don't keep in with her, you will not be able to play with your other friends. Because she is the leader of the group. I wish she wasn't such a bully.

THE SHOW (G)

The other day we were swopping desks. Ava wanted to swop with Emily. But Emily said. 'No, then I would have to sit next to—'. No one wants to sit next to Sophia. It's really mean. Even Dana is mean to her, and I didn't think Dana was like that. Sophia said that she really liked this show on television and Dana said, 'I hate that show. How could you like that show? It's really so, so bad. Anybody who likes that show must be a really sad person.' And Sophia went quiet. So I said to Dana, 'Well I like that show. And how come when I was at your house the other day you said you liked that show too, Dana?' When Dana walked off Sophia said, 'She probably doesn't like that show anymore just because I said I liked it. It doesn't matter.' But she looked so sad. I really thought she was going to cry, but she didn't. What does it matter whether you like that stupid show or not? They just all want to be mean to her.

COVERING UP (G)

The thing about Grace is that while she is the bully and everybody knows she's the bully—all the children anyway—she is really clever about covering it up. How? Crying. She cries a lot. And she looks so sweet. So whenever someone tells on her, the teachers don't believe them. They think 'How can that sweet looking little girl be a bully?' She cries about once every day if she doesn't get her way. So whenever the teachers see her, she's always crying. So it's always 'poor Grace'. But she can be so mean when the teachers are not around. She is really cool and is always the centre. But if you don't do what she wants, she gives you these horrible looks or she'll grab someone and run off with them. And then she won't speak to you at all. She'll get other people to ignore you. It's really hurtful. I asked Julie once why she allowed Grace to make her ignore people. Julie said that if she didn't do what Grace wanted, then she would have the same done to her. And she hates being ignored. So we all try to stay in with Grace and that makes her think she is popular, and she's the leader. But the odd thing is that nobody really likes her.

PICKING FIGHTS (G)

There's a girl in our class who is always picking fights. Then if you cross her, she calls you rude words. One day I was sitting in the playground and she came and sat next to me. She'd been crying because she'd had a fight with someone. But she started it. Then she tries to make you feel sorry for her by saying that she has a bad time at home. She said to me 'I hate the class. They can be talking to you one day but the next day you do something wrong and nobody talks to you.' She says that, but she is the one who does it most to other people. That's what people don't like about her. And she is always pushing to the front. She calls girls fat cows and bitches and things like that. She said to one girl 'You're jealous of me' when this girl wasn't at all. She makes people cry literally every day. But you can't tell anyone because if you do she will start a fight with you or not talk to you for a week. Then maybe no one else will talk to you either. That's the worst thing. Someone called her a bully once, but she said that bullies were people that beat others up. And even if she was a bully, it was only because she'd had it done to her.

LOSER (B)

When I went home last night I asked my mum, 'What's a loser?' She said, 'Why?' 'I just want to know, that's all.' My Dad said, 'Someone who can't stick at a job'. My sister said, 'An unlucky person.' My sister is really sweet and takes pity on everyone. Once she gave her sticky bun to a tramp. My brother said, 'A jerk. A total scumbag.' That's probably why it feels so bad to be called a loser. It's just a word, isn't it? But the minute you are called one by someone at school, everyone avoids you. It's like you've got some infectious disease. And instantly you feel like you are going to throw up. Maybe the word should be banned.

LIES (G)

Jenny came up and sat beside me the other day. Jenny is one of the coolest girls in the class. She always has this big crowd around her and they do everything that she wants. The rest of her gang were on the other side of the playground so I thought maybe she'd had a fight with someone. She said, 'Is it true that your mum and dad have separated?' I didn't know what to say. I said, 'no.' 'Oh,' she said, 'someone told me they had.' But then my eyes filled with tears. My mum and dad don't even argue. Why are they separating? I'm thinking, is it true? She said, ' So they're not.' 'No.' 'Well I didn't say they had, did I. Someone else did.' 'Who did', I asked? But then she got up and walked off and went back to join the gang. They were all laughing their heads off by this time. It's awful thinking that people are spreading rumours about you. Particularly when they're not true. They do it all the time to people they don't like. I couldn't think of anything else all afternoon. What would happen to me if mum and dad got divorced? Someone said, 'Why are you crying? Is it because your mum and dad are splitting up?' When I went home I asked my mum 'Are you and dad separating?' She said, 'Who on earth made up a wicked story like that? They made that up just to hurt you.'

TWISTING THINGS (G)

Emma said in front of Hannah, 'Sarah said she didn't like the way you were always swearing.' Hannah was just standing there and the others were all around, so I couldn't deny it. But it wasn't exactly what I said at all. Emma had been really nasty about her and I'd tried to stick up for Hannah. Then Emma said something like, 'Oh, so you like her, do you? She's your best friend, is she?' and I said, 'Yes, but not when she swears, which she does quite a bit.' Then she drags Hannah up to me in class and says that. It was so embarrassing. Hannah stormed off. The others went with her. No one spoke to me at all after that. But that's what bullies do all the time. They take something you've said and they exaggerate it. Sometimes it's just changing a word or two, or an expression. That's the way they turn your friends against you. And because it's close to the truth, you can't deny it or they call you a liar. So you can't win and they know that. It comes out as if you are really awful. You spend ages thinking back on every little thing you've done or said. Or, if they are snubbing and ignoring you, they will go and tell other people that you are snubbing and ignoring them. They twist things all the time so that you always end up looking like the bad guy and no one will take your side.

BULLIED (B)

It's always me that they pick on at school. Then it's not just at school. When I go home, I get it too. I haven't done this or I haven't done that. So I know it's me. It's my fault. But I don't know what to do to stop people picking on me. People say things like 'You bug me for this' or 'You don't do that'. And I listen. I listen to what they have to say—well some of the time. I listen to them so that I can change. It's not even just the big guys. It's everyone. You think, I'll start going around with a different crowd. So you pick someone who is completely uncool, so uncool that nobody wants to be with them. Or just a younger crowd. Because you're older, it should be easier. But it's not. It's fine for a while and then they start sniggering at you. And treating you badly. For example, you're nice to someone, and then they'll do something all of a sudden like ignore you completely or clap their hands in your face or something. I've even tried to copy cool people, but that didn't change things a bit. I guess I'll always be like I am. The only time when I'm happy is when I'm on my own. Then someone'll say, 'What's the matter, man? Why you on your own?' And I tell them and they say, 'You bring it on yourself, man.' I wish I were invisible.

JOE (B)

They say that bullying is bad but everyone does it. Not like we saw in the video they showed us school with people being kicked and punched. At our school they do it in different ways. They do it for kicks, really. Either that, or if you've got something somebody else wants, you will be bullied for sure. And no one will help you. Take Joe. He's not that bad, really. He's a bit of a loud-mouth, full of himself. But he can get other boys to do anything he wants. He just says, 'Tell me the answer to that sum' and they tell him. 'Give me that pen,' and they give it. 'No one is allowed up this end of the classroom.' You don't go. He scares everybody. All because of his reputation. They say, 'Who's going to be leader this time?' But it always ends up Joe. That's why everyone in the gang supports him. He puts himself about as being the big guy, the leader, and they fall for it. Everyone wants to be in with him. And so he gets his way. And the more he gets his way the more his head swells. (*PAUSE*) The more he does, the more the class thinks of him. You can't blame Joe, can you? (*PAUSE*) I don't reckon he would ever do anything really bad (*PAUSE*) but recently he's been threatening some younger boys.

BIG

People only really want to know you when you are big. It goes like this. The ones who get picked on at school are always the ones that can't stand up for themselves. It is not that they are small; it's just that they don't fight back. If they did, they probably wouldn't get picked on as much. (*PAUSE*) They say that picking on people is bullying and bullying is bad but you've got to do it if you want to be big and everyone wants to be big. Otherwise you're left on your own. Then someone begins picking on you. So everyone is the same at my school. Big people have got real power. If a big person slags people for nothing, who's going to stand up to them? You've got to be bigger than them to do so, and no one thinks they are. So they fall in with them—copy them. They even find it funny. They start slagging the same people and before you know it, everyone is doing it. It gets to be quite good fun. So there ends up a whole crowd of you and if you're the leader it feels really good. So then you go looking for people to slag, really. Before you know it, you're really good at it. And you've got this whole crowd of people behind you who'll do anything you want them to just to stay in with you. It makes you feel really powerful like you are famous. It's great. It makes dull school fun.

LEADER (B)

Some people say I'm a bully but I don't think I am. But, thing is, you're not going to stay a leader if you let people walk all over you. So you have to do things. (*PAUSE*) I don't do anything that bad. I might get people to walk around and bump into the nerdy people, that sort of thing. But then the nerds are usually asking for it. Sometimes people are just looking to be picked on. It's as if they like it. Then they go and tell on you, but when they do things really hot up. I get into trouble over it and that means we—me and the gang—can pick on them even more. You can see it on their faces. They know they've got you into trouble and you've got to leave them alone, but only for a bit. It's always the same. They're all smug at first like. 'See? I got you into trouble'. Then when they see you're going to get them again, only this time harder because they've told on you, they get really scared. I get a buzz out of knowing I can frighten people if I want to. Guess what? It seems to make other people like me more. True. Anyway it's good fun picking on little windbags. When you walk through the school you feel special. You know people are aware of you, looking up to you. You're number one. Then it doesn't matter that you're not clever.

POPULAR (B)

If there is any trouble in the class, it is usually blamed on me because they know I can stand up for myself. I don't care about getting into trouble with the teachers whereas some people are like 'Wow. I got into trouble. What is that going to do with my marks?' And I'm always called a bully. I don't see what is so bad about being called a bully. I'd rather be a bully than be bullied. And you've got more power, which is what it is all about, really. Bullies are really popular. Even though you go around slagging for nothing, pushing, tripping, that sort of thing everyone wants to be with them. People want to keep on the right side of you. You ask them' Can I sit there?' 'Sure.' 'Give me your sandwiches.' 'Sure.' It's really amazing what you can get away with. And power makes you feel really important. People don't tell on you because (*PAUSE*) they'd get it even more if they did. And who cares anyway? But who cares about all that? Everyone in the class is smarter than me, so why should they worry?

CHANGING (B) (G)

The worst thing is changing for PE. The changing rooms are the worst places in the universe. PE is bad enough but changing your clothes in front of people is the really scary bit. Once they pulled my pants down in public. That was awful. They were all laughing, so I had to pretend I took it as a joke. Some joke! Usually I get to the changing rooms early so that I can get a peg near the end. That way when you take your clothes off you can turn into the corner and no one can see you. But yesterday I was held up because the teacher asked me to collect the history books. By the time I got to the changing room there was only one space left in the middle. There was a lot of noise. I was pulling a tee-shirt over my head when someone made the same old remark about my breasts. About how I should wear a bra. 'Cor, they're bigger than my mum's. Someone says it every time we have PE. Yesterday I got this great idea. Maybe I could do extra training after school. If I was better at sport, then maybe the bullying would stop. Then just as I was having this aspiration my trainer stuck to the wooden floor, and I fell. I'm always doing silly things like that. Everybody laughed, and it was really loud. I hate gyms because they echo. Then when I came out I found all my books and papers on the wet floor of the shower.

MUM'S ANGRY (G)

I hated being late. But mum was always running late. Then sometimes she wasn't there at the end of the day. So I didn't get picked up. It was really bad and I couldn't tell anyone. I knew if she wasn't there she'd been drinking or doing drugs. I didn't want anyone to know. Once one of the mums said something to her—I didn't hear what it was—probably about her being late and she started screaming and shouting at her. It was so embarrassing. And she used to hit me a lot. Once she pinned me to the floor and started kicking me. She was angry because I asked her not to drink. She was laying into me. I rolled over. I buried my head in my hands and I was crying. Then when I got up, she blocked the door and wouldn't let me leave. It was horrible. I said 'Mum please let me go.' She said, 'You can't leave. You can't. I'm sorry. I'm sorry.' I wanted her to love me so much. We went to McDonalds after that and she bought me a Happy Meal. Like she felt bad about what she'd done. Anyway, we never had much to eat in the house. Just bread and stuff and it was covered in green. But I hated to see my mum cry. And she cried a lot. If she didn't have me, she wouldn't have had anyone. And sometimes when we are together she can be really nice and funny. I love those times. Yeah, I really love those times because when she's like that we laugh about really silly things.

DAD'S SCARY (G)

My parents split up when I was young. When my mum got with another bloke I was happy for her. I liked to see her laughing. She said to me 'Why don't you go and visit your Dad?' So I did. For a while it worked ok because my Dad used to take me to the park and tell me about his job. He was a security guard and he had some really cool stories. But he lived in this one room. I asked him why he lived in such a small place and he said that that was all he could afford. Then one night we went out to the cinema and I texted mum to say I would stay over at Dad's. Dad only had one bed so I slept with him. When I woke up in the night, he was touching me. I was terrified. I didn't know what to do. You know, he was my Dad. He had a really bad temper, and I was scared of him. I cried so much but he wouldn't stop. When I went back to my mums, I wanted just to sit beside her. She asked me 'What's the problem?' 'Has your Dad been saying things about me?' 'Have a good time?' I didn't want to tell her about it because I just wanted it to go away. I didn't want to think about it. The next time she told me to go and see my Dad, I said I couldn't because I didn't feel well. I never want to go back there again. Maybe one day I will tell someone what happened. Maybe even her. But not now.

I'M A BULLY (G)

I used to be good friends with Holly. But then last year we fell out. That stuff happens all the time and always the group will side with someone. They'll either go with the one who's having the hard time. Or they'll turn against you. I was the one having the hard time, but they still turned against me. I wanted to be Holly's friend. But she always caused the upset. She's a moody cow, really. And she makes things up. Sending me nasty messages and then going on Facebook and saying that I hit her. Or that I screamed in her face. This is how we ended up fighting. People believed her. She said, 'Now, you've got everyone against me haven't you?' Hello? Me? I never did a thing. But because she's small, and she looks for sympathy, the group got behind her. They always pick sides. And if they are against you, then you can't do anything right. Now they are calling me a bully. And I got into trouble because of it. I tried to have it out with Holly and the teacher said that I was being aggressive. Everyone has dropped me. They're no longer my friend on Facebook. They look the other way when I walk in the room. All over nothing. It's made me really depressed.

PLAY FIGHTING (B)

We were just play fighting. We do that all the time. And then Dennis comes running in to join in. Hamid is on the floor rolling around. Then Dennis kicks him but it's only in fun. But when he kicks him it hits him in the head. Hamid holds his head. He gets up and goes off crying. He knew we were joking, he should have done. Then we were all laughing, and I turned round and kicked Dennis back in the legs. Hamid has gone off in tears. He must have gone to tell his brother. Next thing the Head's stormed into the classroom. Hamid has got his brother with him. His brother looks at me as if 'You'll wait'. The Head wants to know about the fight. Who started it? We were just playing fighting. I tell him that. The next thing we are being told that we might be excluded. It was Dennis who kicked him in the head, anyway. But because I was the main one I'm getting all the grief. When I left school Hamid's brother was waiting with his back against the wall. He had his mates with him. I knew he was waiting for me. So I managed to duck round the back. Now I'm walking around watching over my shoulder not knowing whether I am going to be thumped or whatever. It was all over a bit of playing around.

SHE BEGAN IT (G)

Leila is really good on the internet. She has a real knack for it. She writes all these messages against me on Facebook and she draws me into writing things back about her. Next thing she's deleted her messages. But she's also posted all the stuff I've put up about her on to her mates. That's how the net works. Of course they all think it is me who is the bad one. And it's just not true. It's just that she's much better at this chat stuff than me. I have to learn how to edit my stuff out. My mum says not to be drawn into these things. Because she says she can tell what Leila is up to all right. Then my mum has gone and fallen out with her mum over it. Leila's Mum says to my Mum, 'Look for yourself, you can see what your daughter puts up on the social media'. Then the teacher gets involved and says that what I'm doing is called cyberbullying. And it's Leila who started it. I think she gets a kick out of winding people up on the net.

THEIR FAULT (B)

Some kids just want to be bullied. Sam's one of them. He knows he can get away with it because he's the smallest in the class. I asked him 'Pass us that pen' and he said 'No.' I said "Pass us the pen' Again he says 'No.' No explanations. 'Why can't you pass us the pen? It's right by you.' 'Get it yourself' he said. And then I lost it. Why does he say that? Why can't he just pass the pen? It was right by him. My head was spinning; and I felt this welling inside. Everything happened so fast. I got up, and I grabbed him and I threw him against the wall. Then he cried out and rubbed his arms. Afterwards I felt a bit bad because he was looking like he was about to cry. He didn't come to school the next day. Then everyone was talking about him and laughing at him. Mimicking how he talks. Turns out Liam said he told Sam he was scared of it. He told him to stick up for himself and Liam said to him he wasn't going to back him against me. And then I felt really bad because maybe that's what he was trying to do. When he came back to school the next day I went up to him. He looked really scared when I did. I said 'Sorry, mate. If you'd just passed me the pen.' He looked down. I don't like him. But I felt bad about it if he was trying to play the strong guy.

DAD'S A BULLY (B)

Sometimes I pretend to be ill. It's quite easy to do. I just pull this face, and….. Or this one….I always get away with it. Now they say at school I suffer with really bad headaches because I overhead the teacher in the hall. But I don't, really. I like being at home with my mum. It's not that the other kids aren't fun and all that but they wouldn't understand what it's like to be me. I don't want them to know. I wish I had a father like Pete's Dad. He is just so cool. I can't imagine him doing what my Dad does. My Dad once kicked the door down because my brother wouldn't let him into his bedroom. He's really that strong and scary. I wouldn't tell Pete's Dad about it because I would hate my Dad to turn on him. He could. I've seen my Dad punch a hole in the wall. I've seen him punch blokes at football. Imagine what he would do to Pete's Dad. When he loses it, his face turns red and his eyes stick out and you can see all the veins in his neck. It is terrifying. He doesn't live at home any more but sometimes when he's been drinking he'll just turn up when he's been drinking. Or his girlfriend kicks him out. That's why I have to be with Mum. In case he turns up.

BACK THEN (G)

PART ONE

Everything was fine until Natalie left. Jade and I got along fine but then Jade was always picking on Natalie. Maybe that is why Natalie left. I was new at the time. I remember Natalie crying a lot but then someone said not to get involved. So I didn't. I tried to be friends with everyone. Then when Natalie left Jade turned on me. She kept saying things were my fault all the time when they weren't. At first I thought, 'Maybe it's my fault.' I cried at home. But I kept trying to be nice to Jade. I wanted to be her friend. Then she said that if I wanted to stay in the group, I had to be cool. That I wasn't to work so hard. And that I could stay in the group but I wasn't allowed to play with Hannah and Sue. Things like that. 'They play together, okay?' said Jade. Then one day she came up to me and said, 'If you want to stay in you have got to say swear words.' I hate swearing. I said I can't do that. She said 'You don't have to tell your mum' but I still couldn't do it. 'Then you can't be in the group anymore' she said.

BACK THEN (G)

PART TWO

Then she started saying other things out of the blue like 'Oh, you make me so angry when you look at me like that.' Those sorts of things. 'I look like what?' I didn't know what I had done wrong. She started saying horrible things about my mother. Well, not really bad but just saying, 'Your mother!' like she was awful. I love my mother more than anything in the world. 'Your mum makes you be posh all the time.' I usually had an answer for her, but that time I couldn't say anything. Then the week after my party when everyone was talking about how good it was she said, 'You looked so awful in that dress. Where did you get it from?' I thought I was going to cry. She can be so cruel. I have never said anything like that to her. She knew it was my favourite dress because I told everybody my mother had bought it for me for my party. Everyone else said how nice it looked.

EMBARRASSMENT (G)

PART ONE

Geraldine came up to me asked to see my maths mark. I didn't want to show it to her, but she kept on and on. 'Go on, show me your mark'. So in the end I did. And do you know what? It was better than her's. Her face fell to the floor. I knew it had to be because I only got one sum wrong. 'Well I remember that time when I got a better mark than you in maths and you cried and cried and cried.' It was a lie. I never cried. 'I didn't cry, Geraldine.' 'Yes you did,' she said. She just made that up. Made it up on the spot. 'I did not cry, Geraldine. You know I did not cry,' I repeated. By now everyone was staring at us. 'I got a better mark than you and you cried' she screamed at me like a mad person. She is a liar. She made that up on the spot just to embarrass me.

EMBARRASSMENT (G)

PART TWO

She does that sort of thing all the time. Make up stuff to humiliate me. I wouldn't have minded if it had been true but it wasn't. I've never done that sort of thing. But then she's constantly trying to make me look a fool. Make me lose my temper. She does it in a loud voice too, which makes you feel really self-conscious. Sometimes I wonder what she is going to come out with next which is why I try to keep away from her. But it happens more and more. The worse thing is that it is all so trivial. Little things. It's as if she does it on purpose. You can't go up to a teacher or a friend and say, 'Geraldine's just made up this lie about me' because it just seems so petty. The things she makes up are not big things but they just come out. Like, 'you're not supposed to wear that colour socks' or 'That tennis racket is much too small for you' when she knows I've only just bought it. Everyone looks at you and feels awkward. You feel so stupid. But you can't really pin her down because they are things that don't matter. So if they don't matter then why do you feel like crying when it happens literally all the time?

THEY HIDE THINGS (G)

PART ONE

There are some girls in the class who are really mean. They hide things all the time. They are mostly the girls in the gangs. And if you want to be in with a gang, then you have to go along with hiding people's things. If you don't, then they'll hide your things. Take Hannah. She went off Lauren. So she hid her trainers. Everyone knows it was all because Lauren was picked to play centre in netball and Hannah nearly always plays centre. But no one could tell Lauren where her trainers were because they would be in trouble with Hannah if they did. In the end I told Lauren, 'They're in the cupboard at the back of the classroom' because I felt sorry for her. Hannah screamed at me, 'We were going to tell her where they were. It was only a joke. You've ruined the joke.' But they weren't going to. I know they weren't. She would have had to go to Lost Property and been late for games. And she wouldn't have got to play centre.

THEY HIDE THINGS (B)

PART TWO

There are some guys in the class who are really mean. They hide things all the time. They are mostly the guys in the gangs. And if you want to be in with a gang, then you have to go along with hiding people's things. If you don't, then they'll hide your things. Take Noah. He went off Mason. So she hid his trainers. Everyone knows it was all because Mason was picked to play right midfield and Noah nearly always plays right midfield. But no one could tell Mason where his trainers were because they would be in trouble with Noah if they did. In the end I told Mason, 'They're in the cupboard at the back of the classroom' because I felt sorry for him. Noah screamed at me, 'We were going to tell her where they were. It was only a joke. You've ruined the joke.' But they weren't going to. I know they weren't. He would have had to go to Lost Property and been late for football. And he wouldn't have got to play midfield.

NOBODY LIKES ME (G)

PART ONE

It's not that I don't like doing schoolwork—why I don't like school. It's just that no one in my class likes me. My mum says that that can't be true because everyone is liked by someone. But not me. She said it's just because people have already made their friends. They don't always want new ones. They get into groups and stuff like that. But even if they didn't have groups they still wouldn't like me. 'Best thing, ask someone home to play', she says. So I did. I asked Emily home to play, but she said she was doing something else that day. I said, 'I haven't said what day yet'. She looked all embarrassed. 'What day can you come?' I asked. She said, 'I can't come,' and ran off. I felt really bad. Then I asked someone else, and they said they were busy all week long. When I told Mum, she said she would try to organise something but I said don't bother. It just makes me feel worse than ever when they say no.

NOBODY LIKES ME (B)

PART TWO

It's not that I don't like doing schoolwork—why I don't like school. It's just that no one in my class likes me. My mum says that that can't be true because everyone is liked by someone. But not me. She said it's just because people have already made their friends. They don't always want new ones. They get into groups and stuff like that. But even if they didn't have groups they still wouldn't like me. 'Best thing, ask someone home to go for a ride', she says. So I did. I asked John home to go out on our bikes but he said he was doing something else that day. I said, 'I haven't said what day yet'. He looked all embarrassed. 'What day can you come?' I asked. He said, 'I can't come,' and ran off. I felt really bad. Then I asked someone else, and they said they had football practice. When I told Mum, she said she would try to organise something but I said don't bother. It just makes me feel worse than ever when they make an excuse to say no.

STEALS FRIENDS (G)

PART ONE

It's not that I don't like Lily. She can be really nice. But she wants to be with Amelia all the time. And Amelia was my friend. It's ruining everything for me. The first day Lily came to our school and Amelia played with her I didn't mind. Everyone wants to play with the new girls. The first day everyone is all over them. Then you find out they are really horrible and you've got to break off with them. (*PAUSE*) But Lily wouldn't leave Amelia alone. It's bad enough as it is. Everyone wants to play with Amelia because her Dad's on TV and they've got this massive big house with a pool and everything. So all of us, the ones who like Amelia, we go around in this group. But then Lily joined the group. She didn't ask or anything. Just butted in. And Amelia was playing with her instead of me. 'I thought you were my friend' I told Amelia. 'She's taking you away from me'. I told my mum, and she said, 'You tell Lily to find another friend of her own. Otherwise when Amelia has a sleepover, you'll get pushed out.' (*PAUSE*) My mum likes the fact that Amelia's Dad is famous.

STEALS FRIENDS (G)

PART TWO

I told Lily that we were a group and she wasn't part of it. And that none of the group liked her. Well, Mum said she was breaking Amelia and me up. *(PAUSE)* 'You'll get pushed out if you don't,' Mum said. I thought Sally was going to cry when I told her. But she didn't. I thought she was quite cool for that. She still followed us around though. Then one day I said to Amelia, 'Let's play this game. Let's run away from her.' It was only a game. But it was good fun. Every time Lily came up in the playground we ran off screaming. Next break I saw her sitting on the bench reading a book all on her own. I said to her 'You're trying to get us into trouble.' She just said 'My mum told me to read a book if no one would play with me'. Know what? We did get into trouble. Sandy said she didn't tell on us but I got sent to the Head Mistress and so did Amelia. Anyway, I told the others that Lily told on us. I don't know whether she did or not actually. I felt really good after that because they said they didn't like her because she got us into trouble. Even Amelia wouldn't talk to her after that.

GIGGLING (G)

PART ONE

We're having a sleep-over tonight. My mum said I could ask three girls. I've asked Olivia because she's my best friend—Kylie and Cheryl. I told them not to tell Sally because she's not invited. Mum said I had to have Kylie because her mum's my mum's friend. And Cheryl and Kylie are best friends—they're always together. Anyway, Sally knows about it now. I was in the cloakroom the other day and I asked Cheryl what she was going to wear. Sally was standing right behind her. Then Cheryl kept talking about it in gym. I said, 'You weren't supposed to talk about it in front of Sally because she can't come'. (*TO AUDIENCE*) I can't help it if she heard, can I? So Sally says, 'Are you having a sleepover? That's nice.' All sweet like. Then everybody rushed away to change before she could ask any more about it. But she came after us because she'd to get ready for gym too. We started giggling. Kylie said, 'We're not supposed to talk about it in front of her'. (*PAUSE*) 'Shush, will you', I kept going. But they wouldn't. We were hysterical. Sally was pretending she knew what we were laughing about. She was laughing too, trying to stay in with us. 'I was just talking about what to wear to the school disco,' said Cheryl, holding her stomach. Like she's going to wear her teddy bear pajamas to a disco. Idiot.'

GIGGLING (G)

PART TWO

So then we got this small table in art so that Sally couldn't fit on it too. Thing is, she normally sits with us. That way we could talk about my party without her hearing. It was really funny. Cheryl knocked the water over because she was rushing so much to get to that table. There was this big puddle on the floor and she was trying to mop it up with her art overall before the teacher arrived. It was so hilarious. Sally had to sit on her own so we said, 'Sorry Sally, there's no room on here.' (*PAUSE*) I don't care if she feels bad. Why should I? She's not wanted. I wish she would just go away. Amelia asked why Sally wasn't coming to the sleep over but I told her Mum said I could only have us three. Amelia looked disappointed. For a moment I thought she wasn't going to come. Then I told her we were being bought really expensive presents, and we were going to go out to the Chinese. She didn't want to miss out on that. So she's promised not to tell Sally about it. So then Cheryl starts. 'Why's Sally not coming?' So I told her, 'Amelia doesn't like her anymore'. I know it wasn't true, but I felt really good after that because Cheryl didn't speak a word to Sally after 'hat. Well, she doesn't want to fall out with Amelia. Nobody does.

UP HERSELF (G)

PART ONE

Why do I pick on her? Well, first of all she thinks she's it. No one likes her anyway. She's really up herself. If anybody is going to get the answer right, it's her. I wouldn't mind sometimes, but it's all the time. I mean, I'm not brilliant or anything but I'm not stupid. I know she thinks I am but I'm not. And if she weren't in the class always getting the answers right, then it wouldn't be so bad for me. I don't do really bad things to her. For example, I took her rubber. I saw her looking around for it. We had a test that morning and I felt really quite funny inside knowing that I'd got the rubber in my desk and she was fluffing about looking here, there, everywhere for it. Next day I took two of her pencils. Course, I put them back later. Well, that was part of the fun. It was like, wow! When she found the pencils after the test she knew someone had taken them on purpose. She went white as a sheet. She really thought people liked her. But if people like you, you don't get your pencils taken, do you? So up until then I think she thought she'd left the pencils at home. But when she found them on her desk after we'd gone up to hand in our books- because I put them back when she was up at the front—she went sort of white. I thought she was going to cry.

UP HERSELF (G)

PART TWO

I heard someone tell her, 'Jenny stole your pencils.' I remember thinking, 'Oh no, she's going to let me have it.' And for a bit I was scared because everyone looked straight at me. I was going to shout, 'No I didn't,' but the teacher was looking at me too. But, do you know? She didn't do anything. She looked down at the desk for a long while. I started to giggle. You know, like you do when you are in trouble. Big smile, giggle. I said 'Sorry,' like, 'It was only a joke'. I couldn't believe it. She smiled at me. Smiled. 'It's okay,' she said. My mate said she was crying later in the toilet but I don't know whether she was or not. Anyway, serves her right for always getting the right answers. Doesn't she realise how that makes you feel? I mean, it's not as if I'm stupid or anything. But if it wasn't for her, I wouldn't feel half as a dumb as I do. Anyway, it's fun to do things like that particularly with people like her because she never does anything back. I mean it's like she finds it funny too, but I know she doesn't. She's just acting cool, trying to pretend it didn't hurt her. I think I'll pinch her pen tomorrow but my mate says she hides a spare one somewhere on her just in case that happens. So when she's changing for gym next time we're going to go through her clothes.

LITTLE THINGS (B)

PART ONE

There's a lot of bullying at school. But it's not the type of bullying that gets the headlines. You know? If someone gets stabbed or something like that, then it's in all the papers. But there are people getting beat up all the time. Not with knives and things. They get beat up with pushing or shoving. (*PAUSE*) It's that sort of beating up because no one gets told off for it. No one can say they're being bullied if they just get pushed or something like that. I mean, if you just bump into someone you aren't necessarily doing it on purpose, are you? But you know in yourself if someone pushes into you because they're bullying you. The same way you know if someone looks at you in a 'funny' way. In a way it's worse than being in a proper fight. It's more threatening. You can't go up to a teacher and say, 'He's looking at me in a funny way.' Or 'I know he's got it in for me because he walks up behind me and says rude things all the time.' They'd think you were barmy or something. But you know it. You know it inside. The worst thing is you know you've got to do something about it to stop it and you can't think of anything. Your mind just goes blank, like you're a zombie. Or you pretend you don't care and look like a number one jerk.

LITTLE THINGS (B)

PART TWO

If someone's got it in for you—looks at you in that way—you've just got to stay cool even though your heart is beating that fast. Look back at them. Act like it's not bothering you. Well it sounds easy, but it's not easy. You can feel yourself getting all het up inside and you're asking yourself, 'Why am I feeling like this? Feeling bad because someone is looking at me in a funny way. But you are feeling that way because you know they want to do you harm. Sometimes people like that really get to you and you can't look back at them. 'Best thing. Do not look in their direction.' You're thinking, I must not go over there. I must not look over there. Stay out of their way. Your mum says, 'Yes, you keep out of their way, that's the best thing.' But it's not, really. She doesn't understand that. Because if you don't do anything back then it gets worse. So if they give you funny looks, you've got to look at them back, eyeball them, let them know that they don't frighten you. You see, if you won't look at them they know you're scared. Then they start saying things about you, laughing about you, turning people against you, really making your life hell. Then it's the kicking and punching. But it doesn't start that way. It always starts the same way with the little things you can't tell anybody about.

FEEL SICK (B)

PART ONE

I felt sick again this morning. There was this lightness in my stomach. Mum saw me holding my tummy and said 'You've got butterflies. Why've you've got butterflies?' 'I just don't feel too good,' I said. 'You don't feel good again? You'd better stay home and I'll take the day off work.' 'I'll be fine,' I said. I don't like my mum taking the day off because she doesn't get paid, and she needs the money. 'It must be something I ate,' I said. 'I'll be okay.' (*PAUSE*) I can't tell her how I feel. I don't want to see my mum cry. What would she do anyway? 'Big guy like him,' people would say. 'Big fat guy like him,' they would mean. 'Big guy like him scared?' Mum talks over the back fence about me all the time. I heard her tell our neighbour, 'He's kind of happy-go-lucky guy. Nothing gets to my son,' like she's so proud of me. 'Hey mum, did you know I was scared of school?' So, when do you say that? 'They pick on me because I'm fat, Mum', you say when you're on your twelfth bowl of cereal. 'We'll put you on a diet,' she'll say. Or, 'I go to school each day Mum and I don't learn one single thing because of my butterflies.' Sure I can tell her—not!

FEEL SICK (B)

PART TWO

Then I went to the bus and my heart sank because the only seat left was next to Joe. He did what he always did which was to slap me in the arm when I sat down. Then he slapped me again. I knew he would go on slapping me. Slap, slap, slapping. I deserve all this anyway because I don't do anything about it. I just let him slap me. Sometimes he'll keep doing it over and over like a hundred times and I just take it. I keep telling myself, 'Any minute he'll stop.' But he doesn't. I was thinking on the bus that maybe I should ask him over sometime to play. Maybe then he'll become a friend and get to know I don't like being slapped. But I couldn't bring myself to do it. Then if I tell someone else, it'll get worse. I know that because someone told on some kids before and he ended up leaving the school because after that they did really awful things to them. So maybe it's best to keep quiet. Anyway, maybe tomorrow all this will stop. Or I'll get so sick I won't have to go to school ever again in my life. And Mum will get one of those allowances for looking after me and she won't have to go to work.

PHONES (G)

PART ONE

Yes, I am always on my phone. But then if I wasn't I don't think I'd have any friends. Everyone in class uses social media. If you're not using it you'd be completely left out. I like Snapchat the best, then Instagram. I'm on Facebook. I've got more friends on Facebook than anyone else in the class. You can follow your favourite groups on Facebook and Twitter really easily. You Tube is really great and sometimes there are some really, really funny videos. I find it odd that you can talk to someone the other side of the world. Some people think it's bad for you. Say, 'Who are these people? You don't know them.' Thing is, I do my work on time–mostly. Then I text a friend, check my Snapchat. It helps me get through my homework I think. And I am never bored like I used to be. Mum says that at least she now knows where I am. She doesn't have to ask 'Where are you going?' like she did when I used to go to the park all the time. I even stay in the same room and watch telly with her because I can (*PAUSE IN FUN*) play on my phone. Now she'll say, 'Do you realise you haven't lifted your head from that phone for two hours?'

PHONES (G)

PART TWO

I tried to get my Mum to use snapchat, but she wasn't interested. 'Why do you need another thing?' she asked. But I told her 'This one is different.' It's more fun. You can take a picture and add dog ears to it or take a selfie and stick on something like a moustache. Let me show you. It can make you laugh out loud. I love social media but I used to get really depressed when I couldn't get enough likes. So if I put something up I would look straightaway to see who'd liked it and it if they hadn't I would be……. But I'm not as bad as that now. I know someone who will go to the hairdressers and then have all her makeup done just to take a selfie and put it on Instagram or Facebook. It's that important. Everyone looks at your pictures. Everyone wants to come across as really cool. I do too. I know girls who post all this stuff about themselves as if they are having great fun and going to parties all the time. But everyone knows they're not. Then everyone's doing it. If someone has a selfie taken at the zoo or down by the train tracks, everyone else will copy them. Yeah. It can take you over. It can be dangerous too.

SEXTING (G)

PART ONE

My mum told me off yesterday for texting at the table. She said it was rude. In fact, it wasn't texting. She doesn't have a clue about social media. I said 'I'm not texting'. I was on Whatsapp and Joelle was in a right state. I couldn't say to her I can't talk. Mum said if I didn't stop texting or whatever she'd take my phone away. 'Whatsapping'. She said 'whatever.' I know I shouldn't be on my phone all the time but everyone is. Then she snatched it from me and I stormed off to my room. Ten minutes later she was yelling up the stairs about the pictures on my phone. When I'm somewhere I tend to take a picture to save the moment. So I've got heaps of them. But she'd found one of me I took for Dave. It was only fun but Dad got me to come down. Mum was going on and on. You shouldn't be sending pictures like that. What are you thinking of? She was screaming at me, looking down at my phone. She asked me who Dave was, and I said it was none of her business. And no he wasn't at school. And yes, he was my boyfriend. And then I went back up to my room again and locked myself in. I use social media at the very least every half hour. I thought I would die without it. Everyone is on it all the time. They are looking at their phone under the desk at school, or they'll take it out of their pocket the minute the bell goes. When I got to my room, I went straight to my laptop and checked my Facebook and Instagram. But I needed my phone for Snapchat.

SEXTING (G)

PART TWO

I was really upset about losing my phone. My friends were nice and said my parents were really mean to take it away. When I came home the following day my Mum and Dad were both there which is odd because Dad should have been at work. They told me that they were very worried about me. They were trying to be nice. My mum burst into tears. We sat and talked about Dave and how we'd met on Facebook. They said they would like to know more about him and how old he was. I told him he was my age. He was fourteen. Where did he live? What school did he go to? They suggested why don't I ask him round which made me really happy. But then when I went online to tell Dave he got angry because I'd told my parents about him. He wouldn't speak to me after that. Then my Mum and Dad found out that he didn't go to the school he said he did. When she said she had reported Dave to the police, I said I would leave home. I was that angry. Dave was the only boy who had shown an interest in me. But then Dad told me that Dave wasn't my age. He was an older man who was just pretending to be fourteen. I didn't believe it at first. Then I felt really ashamed because I had sent a nude picture. But Mum and Dad told me it was ok. They said they loved me really, really a lot. And that nothing was going to happen to me. They said they would take care of me. And that if the pictures ever showed up on the internet, then I had to tell them about them. Which they could do at any time. Then they gave me back my phone. I think they are the best parents in the world now. And I will never do that again.